YOUR KNOWLEDGE HAS VALUE

- We will publish your bachelor's and master's thesis, essays and papers

- Your own eBook and book - sold worldwide in all relevant shops

- Earn money with each sale

Upload your text at www.GRIN.com
and publish for free

Yacoub Aljaffery

The Influence of English Language in the Arab World

GRIN Publishing

Bibliographic information published by the German National Library:

The German National Library lists this publication in the National Bibliography;
detailed bibliographic data are available on the Internet at http://dnb.dnb.de .

Imprint:

Copyright © 2010 GRIN Verlag GmbH
Print and binding: Books on Demand GmbH, Norderstedt Germany
ISBN: 978-3-656-89261-8

This book at GRIN:

http://www.grin.com/en/e-book/288945/the-influence-of-english-language-in-the-arab-world

GRIN - Your knowledge has value

Since its foundation in 1998, GRIN has specialized in publishing academic texts by students, college teachers and other academics as e-book and printed book. The website www.grin.com is an ideal platform for presenting term papers, final papers, scientific essays, dissertations and specialist books.

Visit us on the internet:

http://www.grin.com/

http://www.facebook.com/grincom

http://www.twitter.com/grin_com

The spread of English Language in the Arab Speaking Countries

BY

Yacoub Aljaffery

Sometimes during the fifth century, the Quran that's written in Arabic introduced the Arabic language to be the language of the Muslim empire that spread around the world: Nadvi (2003) "Arabic became the official language of a world empire whose boundaries stretched from the Oxus River in Central Asia to the Atlantic Ocean, and even northward into the Iberian Peninsula of Europe. As Islam continued to spread through the world, Arabic inherently followed."(P. 2). Arabic became prestige because of the variety of sciences that were invented by Arabs like Chemistry, Algebra and Astronomy. Things have changed today, and the language that is mostly used around the world is the English language due to the advanced technology and the political power that USA, and the English speaking countries has in the world. Hollywood movies and pop culture have a big impact in spreading English language throughout the world. Middle Eastern countries, especially gulf countries like Saudi Arabia, UAE, Kuwait and Iraq have been heavily influenced by English Language in the last few years. Since Islam has urged people to learn other nations' language for security purposes, English language has been taking big part of the Arabic speaking countries. That desire to learn other languages has increased since the second Gulf war in 2003.

Islam encouraged people to learn other languages so that they can communicate with each other and understand each other. The Quran describes the importance of other languages in the following verse: "And We did not send from a messenger except with his nation's tongue/language, to clarify/explain to them, so God misguides whom He wills/wants, and He guides whom He wills/wants, and He is the glorious/mighty, the wise/judicious." (14: 4). The prophet Mohamad also talks about the importance of learning languages of other nations: "Those who learn the language of any community they can save themselves from their mischief." (Mohamad: 1)

Because of the religious aspect toward learning other languages, and the presence of the American forces in the area, English started to be the major target language in the Arab countries after the second Gulf war in 2003, especially those who live in the Gulf region. People started learning English to communicate with soldiers and to work as interpreters for the US army as well. Zagoul (2003) talks about this case "Language and English language spread is a case in point. The language is getting entrenched in the Arab land especially after the Second Gulf War and the defeat of Iraq, a true representative of Arabism and the use of Arabic. English is occupying more and more room in language use. It is taking more and more territory from the

1

native language." (p. 6). After this last war on Iraq in 2003, many English words have been used by Iraqis that blended into their mother tongue language, Arabic. After 17 years of exile in the US, I went back to Iraq this past summer of 2008. I was shocked to hear new words that have never been used when I was a child living there. Some of the most common words that are used today, especially among the young generation are *cool* and *top*. They use the word *cool* which they pronounce it like [kul], similar to how it's used in the English language. Hence, they pronounce the word *top* like [tob], and they use it when they compare two things and try to evaluate one on another. For example, they would say /haða bet tob/ which means "there is no house better than this house". Before the 2003 war, this sentence used be said as /haða bet jɛmil/. Those words and many more are used now as part of Iraqi slang. These new words and terms are mostly used among the young generation. Moore (2004) talks about how new words start to be used in people's slangs. He says that words start to be used among youngsters first, and then they're carried through the new generation. "There is a general evolutionary sequence according to which basic slang terms emerge in mainstream usage. The process begins with term becoming widely used to refer to a set of values that have special appeal for a generation of adolescents and young adults." (p. 63). This to prove that there are many words we use today in Iraq borrowed from English after the British colonialism to Iraq in 1941 which my mother uses who was six years old at that time, but my grandmother, who was in her thirties during the invasion never used those words. For Example, my mother would use the word /bu:t/ which means shoes, but my grandmother would use the old traditional word /hɪða/ instead.

After the 2003 American war on Iraq, Iraqis found it very important to speak English in order to get better jobs that pay more money. Most of the construction companies that came to Iraq in the last five years are from English speaking countries; therefore, people are encouraged to be able to speak English if they consider employment in any of these companies. Omar (2007) discusses how young Iraqi Kurdish people are eager to learn English for variety of purposes, "After decades of isolation, young Kurds are yearning to learn the most widely-used international language to improve their employment prospects." (p. 1). He refers the most widely used international language to English.

Many people started going to English language institutes that increasingly have been opening in the last two to three years. Omar (2007) talks about the increasing number of English schools in Iraq: "Private English-language centers have boomed in Sulaimaniyah since the 2003 overthrow of former Iraqi leader Saddam Hussein, who had persecuted and isolated Kurds for decades." (p. 1). In addition to the big number of English language institutes, Iraq welcomed the idea of building the first American University in the country that was opened in Sulaimaniyah, northern Iraq, in 2007. Politicians in Iraq see the idea of having American "modern" educational system in schools in Iraq a good idea for a brighter economical and political future for their new generation. Krieger (2007) has interviewed the Iraqi prime minister, Barham Salih, regarding building the American university in northern Iraq, "Without providing a modern education system, this society will have a very difficult time ahead," he says. "We need a university to equip the future economic, political, and technical elite, the talent needed to build society the way we want it: a democratic society, prosperous and at peace with itself" (p. 1). Iraqi high school students welcome the idea of learning English through the American university as well. Omar (2007) interviewed high school Iraqi kid, Kamal, he says "Kamal, 17, said he wants good enough English to enroll at the American University of Iraq"

Hollywood movies, music, and internet are big influential factors on learning English and spreading it all over the world including the Arab world countries."The English language is also widely recognized as the world's media language, and the chief language of cinema, TV, pop music and as aforementioned, the computer world. All over the planet, even people who don't necessarily speak the language know many English words, their pronunciation and meaning" (The Far-Reaching, para. 2). In Saudi Arabia, for example, English language is very commonly used in their daily life. Alyas (2008) noted that TV and music influence and impact the English language of people in Saudi Arabia "Certainly English in Saudi Arabia plays a major role in their lives starting from work, daily life, and entertainment wise. For instance, there are TV, Satellite TV, Radio, Video Games and popular Hip Hop which are taking Saudi youth by storm, and not to mention English is essential in the domains of science, technology and medicine." Tariq also talks about how English language invades every commercial part in Saudi Arabia including banks, shopping stores, and even street signs "Although Arabic is the only official language of Saudis, it is usual for English to be used alongside Arabic in road signs and names of the shops. Printed materials in places such as Banks, Airports, Travel Agencies and Post Offices are usually both in English and Arabic" (p. 39).

English language used to be taught in middle school or at fifth grade for the earliest in all of the Middle Eastern countries. However, in the last few years, most of the Arab countries have changed their educational curriculum in this case, and they required teaching the English language in the first grade. In 2006, Zehr, Ann, Kennedy, and Manzo concluded, "Now the tide has changed. Jordan, Qatar, and Syria have also begun to require that children start learning English in 1st grade rather than in middle school — policies that Kuwait and the United Arab Emirates adopted long ago. And Saudi Arabia is slowly following suit in teaching English at earlier ages" (p. 31).

In conclusion, English language is used worldly today. Many countries use English as an official language even if English was not their native tongue. The US strong economy and its political power over the world are the most significant factors on giving the English language its prestige all around the world. Because of wars and other political conflicts in the region, Iraq and other Gulf countries like Saudi Arabia, UAE and Kuwait are adopting the English language in their daily lives faster than any other Arab countries. Oil companies in the region and business opportunities force the people who live in the area to learn English.

WORKS CITED

Alyas, T. (2008). The attitude and the impact of the American English has a global language within the Saudi education system. Novita Royal, Research on youth and language. P. 39.

Krieger, Z. (2007). Born in Iraq: an American University. Chronicle of Higher Education. Vol. 53 Issue 50, p42-42, 1p

Manzo, Kennedy, K, Zehr, Mary, A. (2006). English now the foreign language of schools broad. Education week.

Moore, R. (2004). We're cool, mom and dad are swell: basic slang and generational shifts in values. American Speech, p. 62

Nadvi, M. (2003). Importance of English for Ulamas. Retrived from:

http://www.geocities.com/sayidulhaq/importanceofenglish.htm

Omar, B. (2007, November 22). Iraqi Kurds hunger for English. Middle East online. pp. 4, 5, 6.

Quran. (2008). In *Encyclopædia Britannica*. Retrieved December 14, 2008, from Encyclopædia Britannica Online: http://www.britannica.com/EBchecked/topic/487666/Quran

Zaghul, M, R. (2003). Globalization and efl/esl pedagogy in the arab world. Journal of Language and Learning. Vol 1. (2, 2003).